Together Still

THE
SEAGULL
LIBRARY OF
FRENCH
LITERATURE

Together Still

FOLLOWED BY

Perambulans in Noctem

YVES BONNEFOY

CENTENARY EDITION

Translated by

HOYT ROGERS

with MATHILDE BONNEFOY

LONDON NEW YORK CALCUTTA

www.bibliofrance.in

The work is published with the support of the
Publication Assistance Programmes of the Institut français

Seagull Books, 2023

Ensemble Encore © Mercure de France, 2016

La Grande Ourse © Editions Galilée, 2015

First published in English translation by Seagull Books, 2017
English translation and 'Translator's Note' © Hoyt Rogers, 2017

ISBN 978 1 8030 9 295 9

British Library Cataloguing-in-Publication Data
A catalogue record for this book is available from the British Library

Typeset by Seagull Books, Calcutta, India
Printed and bound by WordsWorth India, New Delhi, India

Contents

TOGETHER STILL

I

How strange: I do not recognize you.
The night is so dark, I no longer see your face,
Despite this light of different colours
In your eyes over there, so far away.
I understand that you are all no more
Than a single presence close to me.
To whom I should hold out the cup
I do not know, nor do I want to know:
I set it down for a moment.
Perceiving your hands, I touch them with mine—
This is more than enough.

True, nothing is real about this room
Where we gather—you and we.
If there are walls, they fade away
As soon as I come near them. I do not know
If this limpid night is inside, outside . . .
I take the cup, I raise it: it is no more.

And what it contained, have I ever known?
It seemed real—perhaps it was.
Let's say it was a wine
We longed to drink together.

I remember the places that we shared:
Were we there, where we desired to be?
A meadow, and those tall trees before the sky;
Or pressed against rocks, in the shadows?
I remember, but what is it to remember?
In the hourglass, the void quickly flares.
Memory is this well. All around: summer,
An empty land of scrub and stone. I am there:
I lift the iron lid, rusted by the water
Of another century, another sky.
I lean in: it is you,
The smile of so many years in that night.

What did we want?
Only to preserve the meaning in words.
They were our cup: language—
I raise it for you and with you.
Are these our voices? These scattered echoes
Beneath a sombre vault, and then this silence.
Strangers have broken down our door:
They blow through us like the wind;
Our room fills up and empties out.

My friends, this earth turns so bleak—
And even, all too often, so vile—
I don't know what to say. Beautiful, this tree?
But someone throws a child down a well.
This line of foam? To speak, to betray . . .

To betray, since this is still wanting to live—
Even happily, at times. And don't these moments
Offer beauty? Beautiful,
The light at evening that enfolds
These almond trees we planted.
Oh, my beloved friend,
I believe, I almost know
That beauty exists, and has meaning. I believe
There is still a sense in giving birth:
I attest that words have a right to mean.
And yet how difficult it is
To convert this faith into thought—
How natural it seems that it makes us feel ashamed.

And who is he,
This man I see who has come to join us?
Why of course, it's you
Who did me so much good when I was twenty:
I never doubted myself at all—and yet
I needed someone who had faith in me.
I never stopped addressing you formally,
My friend. But I still hear
The hammering in your voice
When you liked to say that the mad
Language of poetry is 'shattering'.
Often, you were wrong,
But I knew the truth in your erring ways.
Accept what I offer you, tonight.

It is my need to keep believing
That being has a sense. And even if
Outside, it's wind and stone. Barely, far away,
A few stumblings of the light.

And hence Plotinus taught
That light is born from the eyes,
That it leaps from them into matter—
That it seeks. And sometimes this great beam—
Which turns, hesitates at times, stands still
To become words, almost indistinct—
Issues from blind eyes. It is moving
To see these empty orbs cast their rays.

I take you, a blind man's hands;
On your fingers, I place
My thirsty lips. Another among you
Was he whose words, stifled
By a quenchless need for the absolute,
Tore with their own beam of light
My sky that was so black for several years.
He knew the kind of suffering
That springs from recognizing
What he most desired would forever
Be refused; and worse, he understood
That this desire was but his dream. Yet he grasped
He must decide this dream was real
In order to give life again

To the woman he loved—who didn't love him,
Though she died from dreaming as much as he.

And these others, several others . . .
It was already night. They gave me books;
They turned their pages. I did not dare
To understand their words, which bored into me
As if they too were an abyss: those cries
From height to height hemmed in by rock,
Those arms flung up towards the useless sky,
Those muffled blows in windowless rooms—
So much, forever so much, of this death
We cannot comprehend. But I would listen
Despite my anguish, and I would see
Lower down—like a child nestled
In the peace of his dream—the sky, the earth,
Linked to each other by the vault of trees,
Still grey from the dawn that gathered
Handfuls from the colour yet to come.
Going out, early in the morning, when all is calm,
When the good is the fruit in the foliage,
And the true is the almost inaudible hum
Of animals waking all around us . . .
My friends, let us understand
That these pensive lives—of branches, of bushes—
Know; that their waiting
Justifies our loving. Let us decide
That the flame of this alphabet book must burn

Upright on our tables, this night still. Let us take the cup
Of our words, even shrivelled, even charred;
Let us drink from nothing—and love
The nothing of star clusters, of white dwarves.

One of us rises, leaves the room;
He peers at the sky above the night.
It is a river without banks: yet its flow
Suddenly turns, over there—as if called
Into the future by an unknown cry.
Should you go up to him
And touch his shoulder with your hand—
No, he will not be startled.
His name,
It seems he will not hear . . .
Turning towards us, all the same,
What's left of his face, beneath the stars.

And I say to myself, it's you,
My mentor, my professor of philosophy—
Who told us, with his little smile,
That he would refuse to shake hands
With a visitor who was famous, but who lied.

You knew how to translate
The sublime epitaph of Kierkegaard.

II

Cup of trust,
Moulded from the clay of major words,
We know full well
That your form is formless. But what does it matter:
Loving proves more to us. In a first day's
Happy illusion, I had chosen
A bluish stone: *safre*. O my beloved,
Let us preserve its beautiful name. I take your hand,
And the river is this throbbing in your wrist.

And with our hands seeking, finding, loving each other,
We have fashioned another life.
The cup is born simply from our palms
That brush and nudge, that overlap
In this clay, desire—in loving, this vow.

Then, in the hollow of the clay, these new eyes . . .
We understood it was the same
Glimmer we had loved to watch
As it welled before the break of day
From underneath the crest—still undefined—
Of our low mountains. And what mute
Refinements in the fiery metal of the vast

Sweetness that would be dawn!
A tree would appear, and then another tree—
Still black. We might have thought, from those signs
They seemed to trace on the background of mist,
That a god of benevolence conceived
This earth—it was so perfect—
To reconcile mind and life.
The ring we never wore on our finger,
Let it be this place:
Sheer reality—sufficient, without proof.

And what we were, was it part of the real?
The chestnut-hull of an expectation, that would split
Some day from its weak, invincible thrust?
Blue, this slope lower down on our path;
Silent, our threshold's wooden gate;
High, the plumes of smoke. The visible is being,
And being is what brings everything together.
O you—and you, life born from our life—
You reach out your hands to me: they join.
Your fingers are both the many and the One;
Your palms are the sky, and its stars.
You are those as well who hold the great book—
No, you give it birth. You raise the pages,
Fraught with signs, from this abyss
That is the thing still awaiting its name.

I remember.
The night had been that beautiful storm;
Then, for entangled bodies,
The bonding acquiescence of sleep.
At dawn, the child entered the room.
The morning meant we understood
That the fruits seen in dreaming were real;
That our thirst could be appeased. And that light,
When it stands still, is happiness.
I remember. Is this remembering?
Or imagining? Easy to breach, the frontier
Between all and nothing, over there.

III

Dear ones, I bequeath to you
The anxious certitude by which I have lived—
This dark water, riddled by reflections of a gold.
For it wasn't all a dream, don't you agree?
My beloved, we truly did unite our trusting hands;
In genuine slumbers, we truly slept;
And truly, at evening, those two peaceful clouds
Embraced in the limpid sky.
The sky is beautiful, at evening—and this, because of us.

My friends, my loved ones,
I bequeath to you the gifts that you gave me—
This earth close to the sky, joined to each other
By those numberless hands, the horizon.
I bequeath to you the fire we watched,
Burning in the smoke of dry leaves
A gardener of the invisible had raked
Against a wall of the lost house.
I bequeath to you these waters, which seem to say
In the invisible—the hollow of the ravine—
That the void they carry forward is an oracle;
And the oracle, a promise. I bequeath to you
This ash, heaped in the extinguished hearth,

Along with its embers, now sparse.
I bequeath to you the tearing in the curtains,
The windows that rattle,
The bird trapped in the closed-up house.

To bequeath, what do I have? What I desired:
The stone of a threshold, warm beneath bare feet;
The summer standing erect in its sudden rains;
The god within us we will not have had.
A few photographs I can bequeath:
In one of them—cheerful
As you come back inside, a young woman
With her child, in that day's abrupt downpour—
You pass near a statue that was once
Our mutual sign of acknowledgment;
And is, in the empty house, our belonging
That stays near us at present, as it awaits
Our need of it, on the final day.

URSA MAJOR

What's That Sound?

What's that sound?

I didn't hear anything.

You must have! That rumbling. Like a train that went by in the cellar.

We don't have a cellar.

Or in the walls.

They're so thick. So many centuries have stacked them up . . .

Exactly . . . Oh, listen!

I don't hear anything . . .

Come now! It was like a shout—no, several shouts mixed together.

I don't believe you.

You have to believe me. There, again!

Again what?

Voices, people talking to each other. Three or four of them. It's hurried, violent.

You haven't had time to hear them.

Yes I have! True, it was short. But it was long, too. All right, a single moment. But endless. A chunk of stone, with its markings, its cracks, all its colour: that's truly infinite, isn't it? These people have been talking to each other for centuries. Here, here.

Here—where?

Here, of course, in this room where we are. Right next to us. Look!

I don't see anything.

You don't see anything! What about those heads? Those two beings arm in arm—no, with one arm around the other's neck? They're coming forward! Passing through us!

Look around you, my friend. The sun on the paving stones, the bit of dust in the ray of sun that falls from the high windows, the beautiful space of this room.

Listen to that music . . .

Yes, I hear it rising—growing, growing . . . Oh!

What is it?

That scream, so loud, so piercing! As if the world were about to end!

Wide and bright, the light of this summer morning. Pleasant, the path through bushes and flowers. The scent of thyme and rosemary—or else it's mint—is really strong today. Insects devour each other on flat grey stones, with spots of moss.

And That, Again?

What is it? Tell me.

A man, a woman.

You think so?

I guess. Those wings . . .

They aren't wings.

True, it's smoke. And that fire, starting up again.
The sky is burning!

I don't see it . . . Tell me more!

A stone?

No, it's too big, and there's water inside—it's over-
flowing!

But it's beautiful. For me, it could be enough.

No, it's too . . . How should I put it? Too open.

Then what? God?

No, not yet!

Be clearer.

Not today . . . Maybe it's a hoopoe?

Like that, not even moving? Asleep on the path? Letting you pick it up, as you're doing now?

It's warm. Listen!

Yes, I hear . . . music.

No, my friend, those are tears. I'm afraid it might be a little child, sitting on the bank and crying.

Hold him in your arms! Put him somewhere. How about that tree?

He'd get lost. So many paths in the trees . . . Forget him!

You think I'd be able to? . . . A turtle!

Come now!

Not a turtle? With those wings?

Turtles don't have wings.

Oh, I don't know, I don't know any more. Things laugh, they laugh at us; holes open in the ground; the sky is falling.

Ursa Major

Is it cold now?

I don't know—yes, maybe.

Have you got a good hold on me?

Yes, don't worry.

I'm so scared! Don't let go of me!

You think I want to?

No, but where are you? Where are we?

I don't know. In the sky.

Are you sure? My feet are sinking into water.

It's the water of the sky.

I hear voices, shouts.

Voices? Me too—I'm scared.

Look to the left. Colour!

Hold on to me, hold me tight!

And those people on the road. Is there a celebration tonight?

No, those are animals—immense.

No, children. Nothing but children. I'm scared.

Hold on tight to my neck. Let's keep talking!

Fire—what's that?

I don't know. The same thing as those stars, perhaps.

I wonder why the sky is so close, at night.

I don't wonder about anything now. I just look. No, not even.

Let's go into this room. Wait, there's water!

We'll slosh around.

We'll shout, scream. We'll understand everything.

You will. As for me, I'm going ahead. I won't turn back.

Oh, don't leave me. The stars shine, the sky is moving.

Farther, Higher!

Where are we? I can't see you any more.

What I see is white. Lots of white. Is that you?

Come closer!

I can't. There are steps; they're slippery.

I'll hold out my hand to you.

All these steps! Where are you taking me?

Look, it's dawn!

Dawn? This water?

Yes, dawn. As you can see: it's red.

Red? No, it's blue, nothing but blue—a very dark blue.

It's red.

Red? I think colours . . .

Are what? Say it quickly!

Men, women! When I was a little girl, the sun rose behind our house. It would fill it, in one fell swoop. Almost naked, we would run from room to room.

You call that colour?

They would watch for us at the door, holding out their hands. I liked red because she was a woman. Blue would hoist me on his back; I bumped against branches . . .

Why have you stopped talking?

I'm remembering.

Those dogs over there! They're coming after you. Don't follow me! They'll devour you.

I'll lie down on my childhood bed, my friend. You used to hold my face in your hands; I'll give it to you again. You'll rise up in stone; they won't devour me.

Climb up, climb up!

Don't look back!

No, I will look back. There's no choice.

Yes, Hello?

Yes, hello?

I'd like to talk to you.

Who are you?

I'm redness—a whole red sky.

Name yourself some other way.

All right: this stream. In the grass, with chips of coal. Oh, mostly lumps, as they used to say, broken lumps. The water stirs them up—it's beautiful. I'm here by chance: I plunge my hand into all these reflections, I pick up a piece of coal. The blue that runs through this black!

And that's my book?

A book? Another time, for instance, you—since it was really you, in the end—were a closed gate. Night was falling, and through the gate, nothing could be seen in the garden; but I felt that an animal—a wolf, don't you think?—was coming and going beside me. I've read several of your books.

Who are you?

Do I know? Do I know who you are? You have the shape of a tree at night, against the sky, when only a trace of moon is left.

And who's that woman?

Which one?

The one whose knees are bare. Who's sitting in the grass, so it seems. The one who's smiling—look.

That one?

Yes. She's lying down now, undoing her dress. She's like a train coming from far away—infinitely far—in the dark. As if we heard its sound grow and grow.

You, Again!

Hello? You, again!

Yes . . . please forgive me.

Forgive you for what? For existing?

Almost. There are days when I feel so close to you. We had the same garden. And like you, on the ground in front of the cellar, I used to fill little iron boxes with dirt—the ones with serrated edges. There were tiny white shells in the dirt.

We had never seen the sea.

But you had your ways of imagining it. A long plank stretched out, though propped up a bit by two bricks at the back. You would kneel, with marbles in your hands, tossing them onto the plank. They would zigzag and collide; they would flow back to you again: that was the sea.

Later, I told her: stay, don't leave me—not today! But laughingly, she'd pull away. Her hands were full of water; night was falling. Our boat was gliding towards . . . where? We didn't know, in that blackness.

You've always preferred words to things.

No, I haven't! I knew so few words. It's true I only had a few things. And she had even fewer.

She? It was night. She would tap at the windowpane. I would open: her immense head filled the window, from top to bottom. I was scared.

She still taps; you still let her in.

I believe in a beauty from behind the world. All we have is badly nailed planks, disjointed, standing awry. You hit them: they fall down.

Star Seven

Latin?

No, it moves too much.

Greek?

I reached towards it trustingly, God knows! But it tried to bite me.

And there, from beneath? A voice?

No, it's just sound.

It's a voice, I tell you. Sound, maybe, but mixed with laughter . . . No, tears.

A voice? More like the night star.

Come now! So full, so restless?

That's her reflection—it's in the water. When the moon is in the water, she pervades everything: the pond overflows; the mad groan. See, that's her head—there, dripping wet. And she's looking at us. It's me. It's me.

I'm afraid.

Don't be afraid. She has two hands—they're soft. You rest your forehead in them: your dreams dissolve. You even . . . embrace her.

Will she know who I am? Even that I exist?

She knows everything. When she rises in the morning, she sets her bare foot on flagstones from before the world.

Does she pull into the station? In the countryside, her sound had been increasing for a while. And all around us the landscape was deserted, in those years— because already at first light, we had our big satchels on our backs.

It's true that she's also the fog you loved, through the grapevines. The bird that seemed to go with you as it sang, flying close to you from tree to tree.

There were puddles—it had rained. Tell me your name.

My name? Do you really know what a name is?

Something like a reflection; the song of frogs in the water, with cries underneath at times, and splashes; and this yellow light that moves, that will grow. Don't tell me your name! Decide that it's star seven and that everything ends.

THE BARE FOOT

Inside, Outside?

I

Cut and run—yes, that way! Where the laundry is drying.

So many colours! This red shirt; those others—blue. Whites in every shade of white. That washcloth left on the grass.

They laugh. They play at being colours, at wearing them. At throwing the ball of colour back and forth. Catching it in mid-flight or pouncing on each other till they wrest away whole handfuls of red, of blue—their breathing fast, their mouths so close.

And now this evening wind, in all the laundry as it sways!

A sheet swings loose. Will it fly away? No, it falls down with a thud . . . Slip between two other big sheets that flap, still wet. Get lost in their whiteness, where shadows move. They head over there, where the sun sets. It's well worth painting.

And as it happens, a painter is there, behind his easel. A golden beard. A straw boater, gripped against the wind. With the other hand—is it the left?—he tries to paint.

This is the 'laundry' variant.

II

And what if it were over here?

A gate, to be sure. They push it open and they're outside. Entirely outside, the great outdoors—flat, unknown, with animals far off, that seem to think of something else.

And here, in front of them, a child—yet another one—perched high on a wall against the sky. He laughs. He tosses sweaters to them, jeans, and a black dress, old and torn.

Put that on, he tells them. They do. They look at each other, and burst out laughing too.

And now, climb up!

There are stairs, in fact, and they climb them. Soon they reach a terrace.

And on that terrace there is a whole new wall, with the child on top again, very restless. What does he do? Guess. He throws some photos down, in bundles that come undone. How sad, to ruin those pictures . . . White, black, an entire life.

That one, for example. Pick it up!

Why, it's my grandfather!

True: a little boy in a sailor suit. He's very solemn because of the hoop he's been given, for the duration of the pose.

The 'photographs' variant.

The Milky Way

Are we sleeping, my friend?

Yes. That sheet we pulled back: it's the stars.

I stretch out my arm. Is that your hand?

Do I know?

Your foot touches my foot. It's Cassiopeia; no, it's Alpha Centauri; no, it's the Virgo constellation. Oh, hold me.

You're my little sister.

I was. All those worlds that drift by above us!

It's the lower sky.

And those boats, higher still! As many as planets, stars. Take my hand, let's go up together.

O armful of beams that you are! And its mirror.

When I was a little girl, at night I would look at the sky. You were crouched there like an animal, ready to pounce. I said to myself, is that Cassiopeia? Everything was gliding by, in silence. Father and Mother had left— to go where? I was alone.

I would call you.

And we would take that little path: it was the sky. I would go barefoot. The pebbles hurt me.

Look at those beings from who knows where, standing up there in their boats. They have poles. They sink them into what seems like light. The poles graze us—we who are drifting; tenderly, they brush your shoulder.

Beings, no.

I hold you naked in my arms. It's the middle of life.

The Bare Foot, the Things

She ventures a bare foot, then a whole leg from the sheets of the garden of Eden. Touches a ground.

Oh, it's cold.

What is it? he asks her, from the depths of sleep.

Who can tell? Things, the things.

The things? What's that?

I don't know. Stones, water that runs over things that resemble stones. When I dip my foot in, it's cold.

Tell me: what is it like, a thing?

I don't know. Like everything, nothing. Inside, outside.

Does it move?

Maybe not. It breathes.

Everything breathes.

Yes, but it breathes . . . in another way.

Oh, tell me! He sits up; he opens his eyes.

Another way? By not moving. By rolling from floor to floor. I nudge the thing with my foot, and it hurtles down the stairs. You can hear it bouncing down those steps, stopping for a moment where the staircase turns—you remember. But it's silent, despite the noise.

I remember. Daylight was creeping through the closed shutters. It was early morning; it was cold.

I heard those noises on the staircase: I was scared.

Don't be afraid anymore, my dear; let's go back to sleep. Why imagine there might be worlds?

But you exist! Don't you?

Do I know if I exist? We used to go outside, it's true. We would walk in the meadow; it had rained. And those hailstones at times, in the grass. Tears are melted hailstones.

I hear noises: I think the grape-harvests have started! Come to the window: we'll look, we'll see. With my foot—oh, distractedly—I'll touch the baseboard under the window.

I'm very fond of you.

And I . . . I'm sitting very close to you on the bed. It's really morning, isn't it? With my bare foot, I touch a cold flagstone.

Voices in the Treetops

Those voices, listen!

Yes—up there.

In the trees? Even higher?

Who can tell ? There are shouts.

No, laughter.

Laughter and shouts, all at once.

They climb; and now, God knows why—or maybe not—Eve has perched so far up that when she turns round, she feels dizzy. Adam, who's followed her from branch to branch, holds out his hand. Eyes closed, she ventures her long leg: the first hand the world has known grips those somewhat dusty toes. She comes back down, cautiously—or maybe not.

I've seen, she says.

Seen what?

Elsewhere. I've seen elsewhere. Very small. Clouds that don't move. Houses.

And she offers Adam some elsewhere: that fruit of the tree. Let's go higher!

Ah, so many branches and leaves, so many fruits . . . They push branches aside so they can reach even more of them, higher and higher. They gaze into the distance, together this time. This is the 'real life' variant.

They won't come back down. Children are playing up there—squabbling, with shouts and laughter such as we don't know on earth.

They hardly pay attention to some stones—falling on them from where, they can't tell: from somewhere still higher in the world. Stones of different colours and sizes, rebounding against the branches, breaking them sometimes. Sometimes killing.

This is the 'treetops' variant.

TOGETHER MUSIC AND MEMORY

I

Far off, they'd seen each other in the crowd;
They knew each other only by that look.
They sat down near one another now
To listen to that evening's music: sublime.

The work knew much about them both;
It spoke to what they dared not be.
It took their hands, to turn them into
Thankfulness and sharing and desire.

From hands that join, the spirit grows—
The music's poignancy, as well: it is
The true that is the simple, even more.

Their bodies are so close: a boat, lifted up
By the ardour that gives birth. And dawn
Is near—their second day, almost begun.

II

And what they will give birth to is a voice.
Like the seedling from the seed, it will
Release itself from matter. Suddenly
A cry, more than the cry, will be a word.

The infinite is not extent, but depth.
It's where a life descends to vow itself
To another's absolute: it is the light
Born at night from their joined hands.

And music was what showed to them
Where light reposed—in which nest
And in which treetop, sleeping still.

Music is the daughter of Desire: he came to her;
She took his hands. In the cup—already spirit—
Of their good fever, she rested her brow.

III

Body that loved the peace of the other body,
Barely visible in those hours before dawn.
Yet more than what is visible: the endless
Measure of the spirit—its steady breath.

I call spirit the knowledge that awakes
When lips unite, in the peace of a hand
Finding a hand in the penumbra—
Not knowing if this is still night

Or the backwash from a nearby shore,
Swelling until here becomes no more
Than the ocean of mingled lips.

The earth appears to shift its chain,
A boat touching the flank of another boat—
Two bodies, gliding in time that has ceased.

IV

The water of the spring was no more
Than its voice; the leaves, but their rustle—
Since night fell. Taking that path, we sought
In vain to start anew what once had been.

It was music's compassion, holding
Our hand, that guided us step by step,
In the dampness of high grasses
Now covering the vanished here.

And all the same, in what no longer is
But that we are, the sheer reality revived
For which our words will always thirst.

Were they merely sounds? Yet their chords
Were still a place—a place within ourselves:
Memory and desire, at last the same peace.

V

We had said: let the path be here. And see,
There is our tree; and high in its branches,
Children play. That is how the earth
Used to press her lips to our hands.

We had said? But saying is the clouds
Tiered at evening above the world.
Splendid, for a moment, their crimson hue—
Yet night has fingers to tear them apart.

Except that . . . See: in music, the other tree,
A flame appears, smiling. It wavers—
And then there's lightning, this peace.

Let's take that path again! Does it lead us
Into night? The night within us has closed
Her eyes. Listen. The changing sky . . .

VI

And it's true, my love: when all is fading,
Something remains. Together, our fingers
Are touching strings, in the invisible.
Our desires, our memories awaken them.

What is music? The imminence
Of this island, that is and does not exist;
Undiscovered, wandering in the mind—
And suddenly glimpsed, almost the shore.

She tells us, I am your other world.
I'll take care of you, all through the night.
Naked, at dawn, I'll go from room to room.

I am, I am not. From not being, what
Flowers is that I stay so close to you.
You will sleep; and I am in you, awake.

VII

Where all was decided: what was that place?
Three times farewell, and then no voice.
The silence grew, rising like a peak:
The absolute or nothing, we knew not.

But the singer was in tears—ascending
The music, understanding by degrees
What it most wanted. She sensed,
In that other world, the breathing of a dawn.

On summits, the sky can be a rose. It is
Snow. Or else it is this child, desired
By the mind from century to century.

The final sounds took him in their arms;
Nothing could be heard but his faint breath.
The voice was dying; song had given birth.

POEMS FOR TRUPHÉMUS

The Room, the Garden

I

This room, closed
Since before time began. Furniture, sleep
Speak to each other softly. Light
Holds out its hand through the panes. The vase
Waking on the table is a pallid blue.

Painter, you alone, you who remember,
Can enter this room today.
You know who smoothed, in the eternal,
The rumpled sheets, decking them
With fabrics whose pictures fade.

Enter,
Silence breathes to you—the silence that you are.
Enter with this vinous red, this yellow-ochre,
This blue of other years.
Make them take light by the hand,
And guide it . . . They show it the flowers,
Only a few, in the gold of dry leaves.
On its finger—as its memory—this ring.

You will stay here, until this evening. Painting
Does more than render life: it grants being—
Even if this hand, that in the shadow takes yours,
Can't be touched . . . can hardly be seen.

II

And having lived there,
Once you reemerge, let your work be this:
To look at the sky above the trees,
And then at the leaves, dark-green. Let the deep-blue
Of this bench whose colour flakes away
Come close to a touch of pink.

It's about life and death . . .
And a woman who used to appear, graciously,
At this time of the evening, to read for an hour
In that delicate armchair—before the right not to fret
About the pace of time had ceased.

An hour, almost an hour. It's as if
Something, perhaps a glove, had fallen
From her lap. And as if, not trying to see,
She'd sought it with one hand—distractedly,
In the coolness of the grass.

What's far away
Remains what's closest. What's most remote
In the past still haunts the present hour:
This we know from colour, where nothing ends.

III

Light has nested, this night,
In sleep; and this morning,
It was a world; and towards evening,
It's even this dress, aglow with a touch of pink—
This gaze that asks a garden
To welcome it, a short while still.

Paints, an empty armchair, a book left open;
Under the first drops—large, warm—
The colour brightens. She picks up—is it
A glove?—something in the thick-grown grass.

The grass in your garden, my painter friend,
Has it grown so much? Does its immense
Greenness cover the world that you were?
Yes, but look: the grass is crushed, where an animal has
    slept.
Its hideaway is like a sign. The sign is more

Than what was lost, than life going by—
Than the song on the road, late at night.

Disclose with your brush this shadow in the grass;
Unveil for us the simple essence of the sign:
This dream—no, this gold—
That turns what was into what remains.

A Café

This man and this woman . . .
Their long silence troubles the light:
It touches their motionless hands.
Painter, make their fingers come alive
With a bit of soft colour. Let it be
Like a remnant of day in the falling night.

And then, one of these hands
Will move, will quiver. The table stands in the corner,
Just below the window, where we see
The evening sky that hurries by.

Panes of glass? No, a prism. And its beam
Keeps searching, in the penumbra of the room.
Here, nothing but the world; there, outside,
Hope that returns, weary from its long
Day in the city, who knows where.

Ah, my friends,
Pass on: it's a river by now. How do we learn
To live—that is, to die? Not much time left
For that, when the café is about to close.

So many misunderstandings! But on the canvas
That seems unfinished, these empty glasses
Shine a little, even so. Perhaps it's the single
Ring of two lives that merge into one.

The Paintings

Oh yes: it's you, colours; it's you, light.
You're there when he opens his eyes, before
Day breaks. Near him, you have kept watch
In the night, and throughout the night.

And with your hands you stirred this water,
Dream, forming waves that rippled outwards:
The circles of a secret that you, his dear ones,
Sensed in him and made yours.

Earth is but the overflow of dream,
A garment that moves along her body:
Of one who may perish, but never ends.

Mysterious, these folds. What they were
Is the evening sun behind the trees—is,
As it opened, the almond of the unseen.

Other Paintings

For a final time, the room, the garden.
Into the alcove, a bit of light has slipped.
Can colour, this courage of survivors,
Grant new life to that which is no more?

Elsewhere, in paintings that don't exist,
A tree grows at the centre of two bodies
The painter wanted almost interfused.
A tree—no, several, an entire earth—

And in them, these colours: which teach us
That life knows nothing of perishable worlds.
That it hovers above, that it protects
Everything we love, and that loves us.

Blue, says dark red, come here, next to me.
Let us intertwine, so we imitate life.
No, so it rises, reborn from our ashes:
And let there be our daughter, the light.

Light, in an Empty Room

I imagine I come back—where, I cannot say.
This is a place both intimately known
And alien to me. Did I live here?
No . . . I have left no trace

And I am infinitely sad . . . But the light
That still dwells in this room today
Rises, comes to me. See, we've grown old,
She tells me; I no longer promise much

For your future life; I'd no longer have you think
That life and death are the selfsame rose
Flowering, in the morning,
When two bodies wake and intertwine anew.

But let us speak. I must tell you of your night,
And how welcoming it is, thanks to me.
I've pulled back the blanket of my sleep:
I uncover my body, and all its stars.

This sun, in the empty room, is night:
Accept that in light, you must grope.

Enter, so your eyes will open wider—
Even shed beams of light.

True, where we are, you no longer know:
But what your fingers touch . . . it breathes.
To my breath, surrender your lips
Before falling asleep, your hands on me.

The sun we woke to long ago, were it not
Already this grand sharing, would be nil.
How did you live? For your mirror, use
The window, the bed of this empty room.

BRIEFWEGE

After the Fire

Is it still a church? These pilasters
Have wavered in the fire's embrace.
Their summits are but blackened plaster now:
Angels and fruits have shut their eyes.

And the nave is deserted. Half-nude,
The statue of a saint keeps her vigil alone.
On her the fire has also done its work.
Outside, even so, the city with all its noise.

Whoever despairs should enter here: more than a god,
This absolute that wandered in the flame;
Almost being, this wind that caught

In the calcination of a light.
Love this sanctuary, my friends:
Where signs unravel, it's almost dawn.

Nisida

Nisida, a rock, a clamour of rough seas
And storms that crash against the dreams
Of those who sleep here with feet bound,
Eyes open on their childhood's remains.

To dive into that sound, to swim
To another world. Nausicaa
Playing trustfully along the shore . . .
Love to dream! This is a key

When all others that unlock the self are lost,
Whose doors a luckless birth has turned to iron.
For to dream is beauty attempting to be

And beauty is to love: it is truth
That will take you in its arms—even here,
Where to desire is a little like being free.

Briefweg, in Warbende

What I've picked up is a letter—tossed
Yesterday into the grass, beside the path.
It has rained: the pages are stained with mud;
Ink overflows from the words, illegible.

And yet the iridescence of these signs,
Decomposed, now is almost light.
The downpour has drenched a promise;
The ink has become a puddle of sky.

Like this, let us love the words of the clouds:
They too were a letter, and our lure;
But light redeems them by passing through.

Shall I try to decipher these phrases? No:
They are more to me, by coming undone.
I dream that night is the breaking of day.

PERAMBULANS IN NOCTEM

I

In the Painter's Studio

In the painter's studio '*at the very witching time of night*'. So deep into the night, what better can I do than venture further, step by slippery step, on their worn stone with reflections of the moon, to where my painter friend has been working all day long?

Groping along, I've found the second door; I've pushed it open, I've gone in. The darkness is almost total. I sense only vaguely that a very rough wall, to my right and within my reach, seems to rise to an infinite height: perhaps into a sky—starless, like one of those that exist in the worlds of here, so numerous. I touch the wall, I press up against it; it helps me proceed with care, as I must because I know the studio is quite cluttered—easels, tables, cans of paint left open on the floor. And also, here and there, formless piles of damp cloth.

But what's this, bumping into me? It's alive: against my hand I feel a wooly back, fairly tall. I must have scared this ewe, because she hops to one side, with a bleat that in this darkness sows alarm. Everywhere, near and far, there's a trampling: I seem to hear jostling, with lowing this time, and braying; and here or there a shrill cry stands out from the sad, simple hubbub of all these invisible lives. My painter friend, could you be a portraitist, then? If I can find a light-switch and turn it on, will I see those heads lifted before me—no, snouts, huge ears pricked, numberless eyes staring at me—with that ceaseless fear, and astonishment at not comprehending, which are the lot of life?

Yes, but this light—where is it? I feel I'm on a sand bank, where the warm water of unfurling waves beats nearby: I hear them, I inhale their smell . . . I stretch out my hand, along the wall. Is this a table, with pencils, sheets of paper? No, no.

Painter, your gestures have always been so cautious, so as not to let the world grow old. Looking straight into colour, making cut-outs—blue, green—you brought your scissors to bear on life, death, desire, childhood. You let all kinds of dawn arise in the thickness of the leaves: and each time it was unexpected, it was reassuring, it was beautiful. Ah painter, my friend, you truly do exist! The proof is this overcoat, black perhaps, this '*inky cloak*', silent, infinitely hard—maybe of cement; without seeing it at all, I touch it on this coat-rack beside which I've lingered, still at the door.

And now two men pass by me. One says to the other: '*The air bites shrewdly; it is very cold.*' He then throws the door wide open, they laughingly go out, and for a moment there's a moonbeam—narrow, but bright enough for me to glimpse you over there: at the centre, in the studio of your endless quest. Where are we? On ramparts. You're sitting by one of those large crenations, your back against the stone, your eyes turned away from this sky, starless indeed. And in your hands, you hold before you sheets of paper whose blood is dripping: it is a face again, that of a god—a great suffering that you respect. But what are you doing?

I wouldn't have known, from this threshold where I was; but it so happens that I'm also quite near you, my friend, and I see that you are immense. A kind of gardener, you undertake to make water flow—there's green and blue, and yellow-ochre, and black as well, to be sure, and red: the red of the evening sky—in the restless creases of this field from the beginning of the world. Water that comes from infinitely far away to rejuvenate this soil that has been plowed. Plants are already growing that as recently as yesterday, neither you nor I would have known. And here's the ewe that had bumped into me: she has come back. Her head seeks my hand; she trembles. She's asking, of course, as everything asks on this earth.

Behind this studio there's a large garden, or park, with trees from another century, and old paths that no longer lead anywhere. At one point, I have reached a sort of pavilion. Three steps up, you go inside: just a small room with a table, where a coil of rope was left some time ago. The coil is undone; one end of the rope dangles down—touching the ground, almost.

The Translator's Task

Translate? The young translator dives in. Those are the fitting words, since he will remain forever young, and this page he's looking at is an ocean—water enclosed. It's true that suns cover the gentle swell of the surface with tiny sparkles, almost lighthearted; but he knows that underneath is an abyss: green at first, then a blue-green that couldn't be darker, soon turning to black.

He's dived in. And suddenly, all around him, there's a bit of vague brightness, where in several spots he notes what seem to be lives. What is this one in front of him? He swims in that direction, takes a look: it's spherical, shaken by vibrations, with a dim luminescence inside. Is it an old light bulb, petering out over a table loaded with books? In fact, a student is sitting there, with his forehead on his notebooks, his arms around his head. He seems to be asleep. The windows of his room are shut tight, but the water outside strikes their panes savagely. What silence!

Move on, with a limber stroke of the arms—leave this medusa behind.

And that other one, glowing somewhat less? Why, it's the same young man! He shouts and struggles, trying to break free from the two grim thugs who will soon overpower him—that much is clear—but to take him . . . where? Rosencrantz and Guildenstern, obviously.

And so, at varying removes, these existences, these lights. Must I decide they're organic—medusas, as I was saying, or octopi? Motionless, while one of their gazes filters from under an eyelid. Or may I recognize them as graceful clouds, halted in this sky below with incredible colours, neither of morning nor of dusk? Perhaps they are only words, only thought? Nothing but a heap of images, bereft of meaning, though neither memory nor will can make them fade? Knots of smoke that spiral in the water, much bluer now than green—vaults the swimmer no longer sees above him once he lithely descends, searching.

My child, where are you? Don't hide!

Yes, translation is difficult. We don't know if we have the right to imagine.

And the translator dives again; dives further ahead, further down; dives again, lower and lower. The lives in the abyss become scarcer, less luminous; he doesn't know if they're endowed with consciousness or not. Polonius runs by, whimpering and out of breath. It's all too much for this fat man—he's going to collapse over there, where he'll have the right to believe he's on a beach of black sand, before a dawn drenched in mist.

Descending, yes, in starts and stops—his eyes giving their all to question the immensity of night. What should he do with this word, for example, in that sentence? The sentence has a rhythm; I thought it was English, and maybe it is. But that word—no, it isn't English. It doesn't belong to any known language: to any in this world. In that verse by Shakespeare, it is silence—shining vaguely, the way stones do.

Descending. From now on, years must pass by before we spot one of those beings, if that's the right word for them.

The translator understands that he will never reach the ground of which he has dreamed. He admits to himself that—after finally finding bright sand under his feet—he will never stand up straight, his eyes filled with light. How beautiful it would have been, all the same—how reassuring, how beneficial—to touch the grand wreck with his hands! There it lies, shattered. Of the enormous masts, nothing remains upright. Trunks full of books have burst open. Are pages still scattered around them? No, not even that. And yet a sentence painted on the prow might be visible. We could make it emerge from the night, using the torch we've saved for this great moment. We could dream of translating it into some other language besides this idiom from elsewhere, from nowhere, that is deep inside each one of us.

A Birthday Party

What a wonderful gathering this evening, in the gardens of this large old house on the Boulevard Saint-Germain! Many friends are here, pleased to see each other again—some after years, if not centuries.

But what strikes me is that a few of them are very different from usual. John, who has come from Oxford, where he studies, is a broken-down old woman, her white hair in disarray . . . a lovely smile. This man with narrow shoulders and gaunt features, whose restless eyes seek mine—it's little Jeanne!—though she's now become that great writer or painter of a century long ago: is it Elsheimer, is it Dante? I see that he is doing me the honour, probably by mistake, of addressing me. I should've expected him to be of noble bearing, with a cold or distant gaze; but no, here are just two trembling hands—except that their fingers clutch tightly a rubber ball, small and yellow: since after all, this lifelong friend is—also or still—little Jeanne in her proper, striped dress, with her pigtails, much too long.

And all around us—how unsettled I feel, more and more, by these tall men and women, some of them masked: they shout their delight to each other in this sun that drowns their voices and laughter, in the gliding of its shadows!

I go over to someone who's standing slightly apart, where the flagstones of the terrace turn little by little into the lawn. Is he young, old, a man, a woman? Will he answer me in French, in Italian, in English? Or in one of those languages from the blue of distances or the depths of time, of which I know nothing? Who can tell? His sweater is yellow-ochre, soon vaguely red-ochre; but already the scarf he's tied on top of it is positively red. Let's wander off, I say to him. Do you see this ragged path that cuts through the peaceful lawn? These high, thorny bushes, and those boles lying within them, almost blocking the way? And now these huge, wind-swept oaks; but also, underneath—far down in the abyss where we descend step by step—those brambles, and the blackberries we loved to pick there, do you remember? Here we are, my friend, in the forest. It's dark—harsh and wild. We've lost our way: we're truly in the middle of our life, aren't we? We'll meet those outlandish animals . . . The lonza, don't you think?

Who are you? he cries, in a fright.

Who am I? Who can tell? What vesture deprives me of what might have been my life? I take you by the hand, the adolescent that I was. You don't resist. I lead you under the tall, sheltering oaks. We'll be afraid; night will fall; those animals I spoke of will be there. But soon we'll see that star, shining at the crest of a hill, and suddenly . . .

What did you see? What did you hear?

See? Nothing. I imagined he'd be here—that I would exclaim: 'Or sei tu . . . ?' Alas, these trees, these animals, even these stones—none of it exists, you tell me. Abruptly, you pull back the curtain of the trees: nobody there! And yet, didn't we hear . . . ?

Yes, a voice.

I listen. What are those thuds, uneven and wavering? Nothing more than children's voices—their shouts, their squabbles in the garden where they play, so late now, well past nightfall . . . Ah, my friend, is it true that over there, just as here, there's no light but in the night, and through the night?

I walk down a path—quite narrow—that meanders beyond the village. Hedges border it; but through their many gaps, I catch glimpses of an enormous plain, tinged by a remnant of sun. It's truly moving, in this land near the Baltic Sea, the way distances become the horizon, the visible turns indistinct, colours shift into layers of silence. I walk on, knowing I'll pass by a house concealed by its big trees; and that's where those children play—endlessly, so it seems. I walk on. Already dry, leaves fall from high branches, a dust of gold. And above me, 'cantando lor lai', a flock of cranes flies by; for several weeks each autumn they gather very near here—the here where I am and love to live.

The Walk in the Forest

Dear Christian, do you remember that long walk we took in the Ardenne forest? What year it was, let's not ask ourselves.

We had started out from Charleville, where you'd come to join Lucy and me in your little car. It was raining a bit as we left the city. But soon there was a feeble sun.

The evening before, we'd seen the tomb again, the statue. But was it really what we were looking for? No, the tomb of our friend—yours and mine—that tomb is transparent: it's made of air; it's a cloud standing still above one of our paths.

And here we are, in the vast forest now . . . With its long roads that sometimes run—or is this but a false recollection?—past gaping indentations in the cliffs: and there the sky is vaster. We gathered shards of slate. I imagined that Ubac was accompanying us, silent as so often. I had seen him coat other fragments of that grey stone with blue, or red-ochre, or dark-green paint, before pressing them onto large sheets. It was for a book where there were also tombs—and above them, several voices that made themselves heard. I listened to their murmur in the dry leaves of another summer, left to blacken on our path.

There was that lunch at Rocroi.

And do you remember that encounter we had, in the afternoon? Towards the end, when the light in the forest seems only to come from almost flush with the ground, over there behind the trees?

Three people—who came from there, as it happened. They seem to have caught sight of us, too, since they've halted; we see them talking to each other. Two men, a woman? We ourselves have stopped moving, as if an animal were there, quite close to us in a bush—ears pricked, ready to flee. What are you saying to me, Christian? What are you showing me in the damp leaves under our feet, or—I no longer know—in the palm of one of your hands, cautiously closed? But we're underway again. And they also, over there—no, less over there than already very near to where we are. We're going to pass each other, on the only path . . . Greet each other, on the way.

A woman, two men, bigger every moment against this backdrop of bright sky from beneath the trees. And haloed by this light—so that inside their silhouettes, how black it is . . . I even thought for a moment they had no faces, nothing on their shoulders but a torch of dark flames, pierced now and then by red gleams. Still, they draw near; we see them better, they're . . . wait, they're us!

They're us, these three who move forward—in silence, though chuckling a bit. This woman—she's you, my friend! Except with a hat I've never seen you wear before. A long trail of mist that undulates above a blue fur-collar, with hints of plumes. And what are you holding in your hands?

And is that you, Christian? Yes, it's you. I can't distinguish you from the person right next to me, who walks so bravely towards those others. But again, what is it your were holding, and carry still? Is it a little basket, a book, an animal—dead; no, asleep? And what of this smoke, all around? This colour that rises to change the sky? I have no time to understand.

Because . . . is that me? This third one, lagging a little behind the other two? This shadow who carries what? Quickly, I look away.

They're here, close to us; they pass by. With a nod, and with low voices, we greet each other—how could we do otherwise?

And did we think of stopping—did they consider it too? Did gazes cross, did faces freeze for a moment, on seeing someone similar? Were hands held out? Faces, hands, frightened, laughing, all astonished at being, not being. The forest up there and everywhere becoming darker—one last bird flying off above this meeting, with a cry of regret? No, I shall not know what you held in your hands, my friends. And what they carried, those others. No, we will continue, and so will they—on this path that luckily, after all, was in that place almost wide.

Hours in This Journal I Don't Keep

7 a.m. I wake up. In my thoughts, all is clear. Questions that seemed insoluble crowd my mind—but through their answers, their solutions, now obvious, more than obvious: light itself has taken a verbal form. The sequence of prime numbers, for example: is it infinite? Of course, and I know why; it's simple: I can demonstrate it easily. I have full access to that interiority of numbers that has discouraged researchers: and what clarity there—a whole wide sky! Another thing. What did Mallarmé mean when he evoked his 'great work'— 'a book, quite simply, in many tomes'? When he was trying to carry language to the infinite degree of the starry sky? He as well was searching in the spaces within numbers. In fact, 'numbers' was his word, but he kept getting lost in them; and now, better than himself, I understand what he longed for. I accompany him in his project, which I relive; and therefore—alas, since I see that it's illusory—I dismantle it, word by word . . . Does God exist? Quick, I must pick up that notebook I make out on the table, grey on grey—one darker than the other in daybreak's reddening flush. Other discoveries are about to come forth; I need to write all this down.

Still groping a bit, I find the notebook. I open it, scribble some words. That reddish glow is from huge clouds that pass before my open windows. But now a ray of sun has slipped between them: it spreads the daylight on my table. It touches my hand, seizes the pencil, discolours the dream. The few words I just wrote—what did they mean? Nothing clear-cut. And what about the rapport of prime numbers to themselves, that secret I had unlocked? I recall it only as one of those shadows left behind when a nocturnal dream has ended, though we no longer know how to give them content or form. We think we can salvage them, can give them a face; no, they were merely reflections on a glass door: it has already turned, and everything has vanished. I was dreaming, then, and yet awake. I was in those large red clouds, as though in the sheets of another sleep.

And at present the world is before me, around me, within me: the world as it is revealed when it shakes off dreams. One thing after another withdraws into itself, shrinking to its appearance, returning life to that other self-evidence, the one and only: a rooster crowing, a dog barking on the road, the faraway noise of a passing car— as if the red clouds had been those big ink-blots where phantasmatic figures lie dormant by the thousands. But if we look closer, if we consent to see more deeply, what emerges from those vapours is the lovely lane in front of the house, with its tall chestnut trees, and the hedge that was planted a few months ago, though it's still not growing well; the gardener will have to come back.

My knowledge was a dream: now I must give it up, and re-enter the divine unknowing. As silently as I can, in the house that is still asleep, I turn the key to the garden door. I step outside. The redness of the sky still casts a few reflections on the flagstones of the terrace, overgrown by grass. Will it need weeding? No, it's good like this: timeless. Now I push open the gate to the lane; it creaks a bit. The admirable horizon of early spring extends before me: slight undulations of the ground that the softest of colours have taken into their kindly hands. I will walk to the point where the road, and the horizon, and the sky all turn together—other trees, all of a sudden, but the same peace . . . And now I understand!

I understand. And how clear it is, how transparent! What was I thinking? Was I still so deeply asleep, just a few moments ago? Of course, those trees over there—more chestnuts, with at times some holm-oaks and other oaks . . . And also those clouds which have ceased to be red—barely a pinkness on two shadows of white scarves, lingering against that hill where there are, so they say, circles of stones: tombs, perhaps . . . And also the grass I crush underfoot, and the lark from under the hedge that flies away at the sound of my step . . . Of course, these lives, all these lives that evaporate from the clear silt they seem to be: they are, and for a moment will still be, not merely matter but signs, in a text that an hour, the dawn, proposes to the mind each day—unfortunately in vain. Signs that are hardly simple, to be sure. The differences among the letters of this language—which, if we could read it, would allow us to be—seem numberless in the midst of their appearance; but here they are, under my eyes, in all the thicker and slimmer strokes of the invisible writing. And between the words these letters shape: what happiness, what beautiful reason that calmly breathes! No more of the formulae, equations and dreams of the past hour. I understand, I decipher. And so I have the task of making these words understood by those who still sleep. Quick, I must find the notebook I take along in my pocket, whenever I go walking.

Here it is. But where's the pencil I always take along, too? I think of another pocket, then another. I keep looking: as if, in my bed, I were turning towards the wall; but the light of the sky is on that side as well, in reflections on the white plaster. And again I hear the cock-crow, the bark, a passing car. I sit up, I listen. What is on my mind? That remarkable poem by Matthew Arnold, 'Dover Beach'; and above all, its final strophe. Those verses about the serene night, the calm sea, but where the sound of the shingle also resounds, roiled by the surf on the beach.

Ah, love, let us be true
To one another! for the world, which seems
To lie before us like a land of dreams,
So various, so beautiful, so new,
Hath really neither joy, nor love, nor light,
Nor certitude, nor peace, nor help for pain;
And we are here as on a darkling plain,
Swept with confused alarms of struggle and flight,
Where ignorant armies clash by night.

Who am I? I see beside me my friend, my companion, still sleeping and slightly uncovered. And I think about what you said to me yesterday, and that I grasp even better now—another page of this journal I don't keep. You were standing at the window of our room. 'Come,' you say. But then right away: 'Ah, it's too late!' Too late? Because already, in this evening light of late summer, what had appeared for an instant on three or four large, nearby trees is no longer there? An extraordinary increase of its radiance—of this gift it grants to the earth. 'Ah love', let us inhabit this 'too late', still so luminous. It's the same as if we gazed upon the 'darkling plain', don't you agree?

II

Arms That Open

In front of the alcove, at the end of the empty room, a curtain ripples in the winds of a broad, stormy sky—a drapery of words, even sentences. One of them is a painted figure: a young woman with a sad face, whose blouse is embroidered with tiny fruits and flowers. Who is she, who could she have been in my childhood here— one among other childhoods? Will she even come alive again? Yes, she moves, her arms open, she leans towards me. But a hand—God knows where; I can't see it— draws the curtain, making these words slip underneath each other. Now there's nothing any more but scarlet— blood, it seems—soaking the heavy cloth.

And what did the hanging conceal? A bed! Where sky and earth lie asleep in each other's arms, almost naked. It's night-time, in fact—that doesn't surprise me—in this house I've returned to after so many years. And Ursa, which appears late in life—the most beautiful constellation—pensively bathes with her beams the man and woman of those seasons long ago.

Here was the sitting room. Beside the large, ruined sofa, two vases of grey glass still hold withered sprays of dried lunaria. How I liked them—those brownish-ochre flowers, those yellow leaves . . . I used to come and sit beside them; to their murmurs, I confided words that I invented. But their scent crumbles under my fingers, however respectful; their leaves shear from the stems, their petals rain down. In a funerary chamber, so the archeologist of times gone by may have seen a king moving towards him, a queen—though shortly afterwards, they'd lapse into dust. Shades, yes; but still glinting in their hands, the masks of gold they'd just removed from their faces when they woke . . . I gather a few of the coin-shaped blooms, I put them in a small iron box. How many times has the sun risen in this house, left empty for so long? How many times has the crimson light of evening spread across its flagstones? I leave the sitting room. Shrilling, thousands of birds of every kind and size collide in the bedrooms; and one of them is locked—all I can do is shake the door.

At the Dawn of Time

I come back to the house of the very distant past.
And I am amazed to find its spaces vaster than I recalled:
this is true of the staircase most of all, which lay at the
heart of my memory. From our upper floor, I liked to
go there each morning and sit on one of the steps, in the
half-light that came through the entrance hall's thick,
studded door. I also enjoyed the coolness at the warmer
hours of the day. And one time I fell there: my father
was shocked; he shouted and took me in his arms.

But I didn't remember the steps as being so wide and
deep, of massive grey stone, nor as sweeping so majesti-
cally up to the attic—even though I retreated there quite
often to read. You don't go up to the attic like that in
ordinary houses. So now I understand that this house
isn't of this world—that it was laid out in a previous era,
elsewhere. And I can almost see beings from that else-
where grouped around a table; under their eyes are sur-
veys and maps, immense horizons of long limestone
hills. They look at each other, absorbed in thought. One
of them puts his finger on a map, right where two little
children, a boy and a girl, seated at the bottom of the
staircase, are tussling over an object. You can barely pick

it out on this old photograph: is it a small animal they were holding like that in their arms? A small life, with jerky movements and feeble cries—and that was part of the body of one of them, or both? Or was it an entire swath of the wide, starry sky? Though increasing, the light of the summer day had not yet effaced it, that morning. I don't know what they held there, and which they let slip away; but I see them climb back up the staircase—now hand in hand.

Nor have I forgotten that this attic—a low framework of heavy timber, hot and odorous, with a floor of badly joined planks—had been for many years the final resting place of trunks, left open because they overflowed with old books, magazines. Many of these lay about in a permanent jumble, but among them I would find numerous issues of *I Know Everything*—the 'illustrated world encyclopedia'. The cover showed a little man dressed in black, whose head was the terrestrial globe. With a finger—how terrifying!—he touches his forehead, his eyes lost in his dream. Kneeling before a trunk, I spend hours reading *I Know Everything*: from the remoteness of sooty photographs, I gaze at the shores of Polynesia and graceful, half-naked beings on the sand— or take fright at rooms badly lit by thick oil lamps; abominable heads had thronged in their circle of light, of whom I'd never know a thing.

In the Other Trunk

—And in the other trunk?

—In the other trunk? Nothing.

—It was empty?

—No, there were letters, packets of letters bound by rubber bands that had long since broken: everything was mixed together, falling apart. And heaps of postcards: countless pictures of train stations, or city halls, or a viaduct—printed in grey, or sepia, or a blurry blue, on pasteboard yellowed by time . . . On them I would also see five or six words, so often the same, written diagonally on the side that bore the address . . . Believe me, I wasn't reading anything: I was digging my hands into the jumbled mass; I was rummaging through the paper, which made a sound I liked. I came back up with photographs of dignified old men wearing a tie; or shyly smiling women, their hair in a bun—and on their bodice, a handsome Holy Spirit set in silver. Alas, sometimes I also touched a hand in there—still alive; it clasped my fingers very quickly, tugging them, trying to pull me into its night. But I resisted, as you can well imagine: I tugged in the opposite direction—upwards, towards me. And soon the hand would loosen its grip, fading back amid those pale, cramped writings; at times I heard a sob.

—This woman, who was she?

—Was she a woman? Yes, no doubt, since when I stood up from that other trunk, under the low timber-frame roof, in the heat full of tiny motes of dust, I would glimpse a woman—oh, just for an instant—seated behind me on a small bench. An old woman, she was. She didn't look at anything, nor did she move. An illusion, I said to myself.

—Who was she? I insist.

—Her name was Petronilla. A great-great-aunt of ours from one of those far-flung villages on the limestone plateau. She ran a general store. There she sold salted cod, biscuits in big iron boxes, needles and scissors—and thread of all colours, and balls of yarn. Suspended from the low ceiling, there were even toys that travelling salesmen had talked her into; a few of them passed through now and then, despite the sweltering heat in that remote corner of the world. Spinning-tops made of iron, red and yellow. Imitation violins . . .

—Keep quiet!

—You know very well that I've always kept quiet. I will die with my secret. The hand from down below in words will drag me into its blackness, and you will never know, my friends, what those sobs and shouts wanted of me—those cries of fright and pain I heard at night in the empty house.

The Other Stairway

But my first thought, upon returning, had been the orchard; at the end of it lies the underground passage that haunted my memory for so many years. A low wall, like a horseshoe around stone steps—that even on those radiant summer mornings, went down and soon were lost in the thickest night. And there at the bottom—somewhere, who could tell?—a narrow corridor was said to open up, with the goal of reaching the opposite side of the valley: that world towards which one would have to flee, on days of distress. All the same, nobody ventured down that stairway, from centuries long since forgotten.

And here I am, in yet another century, at the entrance to the passage, under the same trees as in my childhood years. But the steps I remembered are not so intimidating today. What's more, I see there aren't too many—hardly more than a dozen flat, grey-brown stones, slightly eroded by wear. There's even a landing further down, fairly well lit by a brightness almost like day.

I descend, courageously. On the landing, to the left, a glass-paned door stands ajar: there's a room, with a window that faces me. Going inside, I pass by a little bed that seems very much of this world—it even has sheets, freshly ironed. And here's a table I walk around. Through the window I see the valley, the river faraway. Yet another door leads towards that outside; I'm on a terrace I cannot help but recognize. It's the second-highest of three or four levels in this orchard, that step down beneath the sky.

Ah, how can I explain to myself that what's most distant, most frightening, may perhaps be just this here where I am, so calm? What can justify this way that space has of denying reality, of challenging memory? No doubt this world where it aims to keep me is merely, round about, that illusion from which I once knew how to defend myself, all the same.

I lean against the retaining wall—made of rocks from the limestone plateau, crudely fitted—where the door and the window were carved out beneath the uppermost terrace. To be sure, it's high time that I think things through. That I pay attention, this evening, to what these hills on the horizon, these mists—pale against the dark, rapid waters the river—this file of poplars are still saying to me now. That I be open even to the memory of the plantain herbs we used to gather along the roads of that over-there, for our birds in their cage.

And have I really heard right? No, these far distances tell me, don't be deceived. Bright, lively, warm, fresh, this summer light we offer you—that you've known how to accept from us, since your first day. But somber, damp, labyrinthine, infinite, the chasm that cracks open there, each instant of your life. We are not, you are not. The sole reality is your dream of an orchard, of a morning in the summertime, of these fruits already close to overripe you gather in the grass, mindful of the wasp and the bee.

The Low Door

They were driven out; they wandered all day long. And now, in the thick grass at this far reach of the earth, here they are before a large house, more long than wide—a farm-house that seems abandoned, with all its shutters closed. But look, there in the shed, that low door, almost open! We can force it, go inside. Duck your head, will you?

A door? Through the cracks in the wood they catch sight of some trees—the same as those here where they both still stand, with the same shaggy underbrush beneath almost the same sky; and if the door resists when they push, it's because on the other side it's covered with brambles—like the ones in the world they're leaving, that scratch their bare legs, their knees.

This low door is quite familiar, in fact: it reminds them of their childhood home, and of the big enclosure at the end of the garden. There, in the evening—when everything turned ominous, all shadows and cries—they liked to take refuge before they were called to dinner. In this back-garden, there was a little house left in ruins where they would hide. I slipped in first, and you followed me. We were then in a very low room with a collapsed ceiling, a half-fallen beam. We would lie down on the floor, in the dry, fragrant straw.

So be it! But now we've passed through the door, this low door of a final day. Oh, is that you? How you've grown! Night has fallen, and this head of yours touches the starry sky, these hands of yours pick up strange things in the dark on every side. Your eyes, of an unknown colour, seek mine: how frightened I am! You draw near me, you tell me, 'Come'. And we're going to have to walk, walk a long time, walk until late, in this other world—it will be cold.

We were saying to each other: Who are you? What name do we keep in the abyss? What will be left to gleam—a bit of iron, a pebble?—in this shallow stream close to where we lie down, in the warm straw of a room from another century, abandoned to ruin.

So Many Good Things!

Ah, we had so many good things!

The Pigeon lamp entrusted to me at bedtime, so I could find my way through the cluttered space we called the sitting room. A space totally bereft of light, when there wasn't—as sometimes happened, rarely—a moonbeam through the curtains of the window at the back. Once the dining-room door was shut behind me, all I had left to guide me in the blackness was the delicate, curved flame at the top of the copper cone. After a long, long advance into the folds of night, I would place the little lamp on a bench by the bed, then resign myself to putting it out.

And these cans as well, made of very thin iron: cylinders with slightly ribbed sides that were used for slow cooking. They had contained green coffee beans bought wholesale. Two holes were drilled opposite each other at their base; they were stuffed with sawdust, granted to my impecunious grandparents by the village cabinetmaker. They were lit: I don't know how. The fire would smoulder for a long time under the black, cast-iron pots—right on the floor. The smell of hot sawdust would pervade the dark kitchen, left empty for an hour or two. And at other times the intoxicating smell of coffee, roasting in a stove equipped with a small, revolving spatula, filled all the rooms. To manipulate this crooked iron tool, leaning over the reddish heat, there was someone whose face I'm quite sure today, this evening, I will never be able to recollect.

And also this gap, under the big stone staircase: a hole whose upper part was the underside of some of the steps. At the end of the vestibule, it could be entered by going first through an unlit storage room, with nothing inside but some forgotten planks. I would push the door open, without making any noise. The hole was on the right side of the little room; I would kneel down and light it up with my pocket torch. Seen like this from underneath, the stairs seemed but a single mass of crudely carved sandstone and flaking plaster, with indents and bumps; and across it were some black streaks I wanted to believe were signs, traced by a rag dipped in tar.

Under the steps: nothing; this cubby-hole was empty. And the floor appeared to be of beaten earth, with some rubble. A spider sometimes ventured across that expanse; I would catch it in the gleam of my torch—it would halt for an instant, and then continue on its path.

Perambulans in Noctem

The first house was for ages that cup set over there—outside time, under the rapid sky of those years of then. From it rose plumes of smoke in various colours, trailing off in the indifference of the light. I take the cup in both my hands—these great thick walls, this sombre river faraway, these tortuous paths on the limestone plateau—and carry it off this evening, in summer still. Shall I set it down at the feet of the smiling gods, themselves of stone, who wait kneeling under the poplars along the bank?

No, I walk away with it as darkness falls; the dream floods in, the poplars dissolve and fade. With my lips, I've touched the libation I carry; I've even drunk from it. I've wandered—and now here are grassy slopes where animals graze, where the sun is about to brush the horizon. Already the shepherd is leading his goats and his sheep to the fold: what silence . . . such a peace as I have never known on earth. And here I've reached the place where I must live; I set the cup in the grass of a narrow path, encroached upon by stones. Let our existence to come be this *safre*, this rock of changing hues, here raised compactly in the walls of our new abode—and elsewhere scattered in lumps, spherical at times, spreading far off into the wild lavender's scent.

I look at this second house in some photographs. Who are those two who bustled around it? They're so far away, I can barely make them out at the foot of the high walls. The trees they planted are nothing but light vapours in the grey sky of these old photos we used to develop—not very well—in a basin we found in one of the rooms.

Let me carry the cup away once more, with its plumes of smoke . . . But where should I go? I've entered the house; I roam through its attics, now deserted. Still there, the smell of grain; still there, through the little windows, the entire sky of spring and summer mornings—and near them the bed, the table. Under the granaries is the nave that the god of another century once inhabited. He'd ended up by adding a chimney; he poked at the logs through the night, watching the fire burn out. The wall around it was blackened by soot—that was our first observation, when we entered that other dream.

I've taken the cup, in both my hands. The smoke from its depths grows denser; it hinders my view of where I'm heading from now on, in this night. And I don't know how long I will have to carry it—until my knee touches a low table, perhaps.

Bibliographic Notes

Ensemble encore (*Together Still*) is published for the first time.

La Grande Ourse (*Ursa Major*), a collection of seven poems—laid out and manually printed one by one by Bertrand Dorny, in ten copies—was published in 2012 at Éditions Trames, in Barriac en Rouergue. It then appeared at Galilée in January 2015, with the addition of 'Dedans, dehors?' ('Inside, Outside?')

'Le pied nu, les choses' ('The Bare Foot, the Things') appeared in a few copies at Éditions Trames. The other poems of *Le pied nu* (*The Bare Foot*) have mostly remained unpublished till now; the same is true of the suite *Ensemble la musique et le souvenir* (*Together Music and Memory*).

Poèmes pour Truphémus (*Poems for Truphémus*) was published in 2013 by Éditions Trames in a very limited number of copies. These poems allude to paintings by Jacques Truphémus, such as 'Un café' ('A Café'), and are followed by a page evoking a well-known canvas by Edward Hopper, a painter often compared to Truphémus.

Briefwege: these are various memories. 'Nisida' arose from an encounter with young prisoners—still minors—in the prison of Nisida, near Naples. This poem appeared in *Racconti per Nisida, isola d'Europa* (*Stories for Nisida, Island of Europe*), Alfredo Guida Editore, Naples, 2012. 'Après le feu' ('After the Fire') was written in memory of a visit, in 1996, to Lisbon's Church of São Domingos, devastated by a fire shortly before. Lastly, 'Briefweg' ('Briefweg') is the name of a former postal road in Warbende, between Berlin and the Baltic Sea.

Perambulans in noctem (*Perambulans in Noctem*) gathers together poems in prose, some of which appeared in periodicals or tributes, and were later published by Bertrand Dorny in ten copies each.

The seven prose-pieces of the second part of *Perambulans in Noctem* derive from a brief, unexpected sojourn, in 2013, in the house of childhood summers—a much-loved house, never revisited since pre-war times.

This title laid a hesitation to rest. It has its origin in a Gnostic treatise of the Alexandrian period in Egypt, *Negotium perambulans in tenebris*. And since I wanted to substitute a true night for the shadows, I should have settled on the words '*Perambulans in nocte*', with '*nocte*' being the ablative of '*nox*', as required by the syntax when indicating that an act is confined to a place. Besides, in '*perambulans*', the prefix '*per*' suggests comings and goings in a place closed in on itself.

But I also wanted to convey that the movement of my thoughts in these pages, however much devoted to memories nothing can alter, tends all the same towards an unknown, possibly even a future. It seemed to me that the accusative '*noctem*' would give an inkling of this—a bit as in English, in a similar case, '*into*' would replace '*in*'; or as in Latin itself, the famous phrase '*eo Romam*', from one of the *Eclogues* of Virgil, appears to suggest. The accusative to express transgression, rupture, at the very heart of the confinement that one continues to undergo, is in fact a kind of oxymoron. And doesn't the oxymoron reveal what both of them are—the unconscious and poetry? Two forms of restlessness, equally constrained.

Yves Bonnefoy

IN MEMORIAM

A Translator's Note

In July 2016, the world community of letters mourned the death of Yves Bonnefoy, the greatest French poet of our time. But some of us also lost the man who was our spiritual father. After knowing him well for almost half a century, I am acutely aware that he was the last of my parents—and in many ways, the one who changed my life the most. Our friendship began with our weekly conversations in Paris in the late sixties, and ranged through our days in Rome, the encounters in Cambridge and New York, and the unforgettable sojourn in Ireland. We frequently corresponded, especially when I was translating one of his poems, tales, essays or books. And truly, the best tribute we translators can pay to such a friend is an echo of his words: an echo that by its very nature must be faint, humble and distorted.

In his last months, Yves Bonnefoy asked me to translate what he foresaw would be his final collection of poems, *Ensemble encore* (*Together Still*). It would include revisions of pieces that dated back several years, as well as entirely new ones. We had planned to meet in Paris at the end of May to discuss the project, but his rapidly declining health prevented that reunion, and I was told by his family that there would be no hope of a second chance. I had no choice but to continue with a long-planned trip to Southeast Asia, writing him messages about my travels from different stops along the way—Bangkok, Phi Phi, Phnom Penh or Siem Riep. Every now and then, through his relatives, he would forward me a brief reply; at the end of June, his words took the form of laconic, moving farewells. By coincidence, he expired on the same day I returned to Europe, the 1st of July. It was a small consolation for me that from Cambodia, I had sent him an English version of the opening poem, his symbolic 'will and testament'.

This long meditation in three parts, 'Together Still', gives its name to the collection as a whole. It harks back to *The Testament*, by the late-medieval poet François Villon, deliberately retracing the entire arc of French verse. As Bonnefoy 'bequeaths' intangibles to his heirs—the evening light, the persistent fragrance of ancient grain, or the murmur of a hidden stream—the house he often evokes is Valsaintes. This abandoned abbey in Upper Provence served him as a retreat for about ten years, starting in the early sixties, and the surrounding landscape informs many of his works. In the French original of 'Together Still', hints about it are sometimes relayed by words like *garrigue* (an arid brushland) and *safre* (a bluish stone), characteristic traits of the region. When the house had to be renounced, for a series of practical reasons, Bonnefoy keenly felt its loss—as he averred in the writings and interviews that followed. His nostalgia for its beauty haunts him even in these final poems, written four decades later.

Another setting that comes to the fore in the second half of *Together Still* is a house in Warbende; as the text tells us, it borders on a former 'Briefweg'—a picturesque lane in Northern Germany, near the Baltic Sea. The thickset hedges, tall trees and lush grass form a striking contrast to the dry, rocky landscape of Upper Provence. As the poet observes in his notes, 'Briefweg' means a 'postal road' in German; and the plural of the word, 'Briefwege', is the title he gives to a section that groups three reminiscences. Among them, a letter found during a walk inspires what was apparently his last poem in verse; indeed, all recollections are 'iridescent' missives from our past, retracing the road of time to reach us in the now. Bonnefoy's valedictory book is a lucid meditation on anamnesis as we live it in the present. And with advancing age, temporality begins to move backwards: more and more, the dwindling future is overbalanced by the vast, oneiric hinterland of bygone years.

Accordingly, the chronology of *Together Still* proceeds in reverse, starting with the author's immediate legacy to his family and friends, and ending with some of his earliest memories: the seven poems in prose that conclude *Perambulans in Noctem*—a Latin phrase that roughly translates as 'wandering into the night'. In his

'Bibliographic Notes', Yves Bonnefoy speaks of the scene of these lapidary paragraphs as the 'house of childhood summers': his maternal grandparents' house at Toirac, in the Lot Valley. They are marked by ample references to the rural France of a vanished age: the shy women who wore Holy Spirit pendants or brooches; the slow roasting of coffee beans in an outdated contraption; the mineral-oil 'Pigeon lamp' that lit a child's way to bed; the great-aunt who ran a general store on the remote limestone plateau (*causse* in French) of the Massif Central. Readers will find an array of vivid descriptions of that era in the author's final memoir, *L'Écharpe rouge* (*The Red Scarf*), which will soon be published by Seagull Books in English translation by Stephen Romer.

At several junctures in *Together Still*, the poet addresses important presences in his life as 'friends' or 'companions': *amies* or *compagnes* with a feminine ending —impossible to render in English, though I have tried to suggest the fondness he implies. Throughout the work, other intimates also come and go, mainly writers and artists. Some are clearly indicated, like Raoul Ubac and Jacques Truphémus, whereas others are referred to only by their given names—or not named at all— though their evocations bristle with telling details. After the book appeared in France in early 2016, there was conjecture about whether some passages adverted to well-known authors such as Gilbert Lely, the poet and biographer, or Jean Wahl, the existentialist philosopher.

However, Yves Bonnefoy evaded such inquiries with reticence, leaving future scholars to speculate as they will. The secondary literature on his work is already voluminous, and we can fully expect that every connection will be pursued.

Deferring to the author's discretion, I would stress that—much like the backdrops of Valsaintes, Warbende or Toirac—the exact identity of any person in this book is ultimately irrelevant to the poetry itself. Here the border between facts and dreams is constantly overstepped. 'A Birthday Party' commences with an event that actually took place, leads us through the 'dark wood' of Dante, and draws to a close near the Baltic Sea. Likewise, 'A Walk in the Forest' transports us from a 'lunch at Rocroi' to a stroll in the Ardennes; but soon we find ourselves in the unsettling sphere of Borges—one of Bonnefoy's literary kindred, along with Shakespeare—as three 'Doppelgänger' appear on the twilit path. Again, the locale of 'In the Artist's Studio', loosely based on that of a friend, shifts suddenly from the restive herd of animals in the workshop to the ramparts of Hamlet's castle. In every case, these wide-ranging metamorphoses unfold largely within the mind: in 'Hours in This Journal I Don't Keep', the narrator transitions abruptly from dreams to brilliant insights, then back to 'unknowing' again; yet he also embraces the everyday 'self-evidence' for which he longed, and which culminates in poetry.

Like the alchemists he often invokes, Bonnefoy transforms everything around him through his own poetic vision, with its 'reflections of a gold'. Even so, as with the fire-scarred church he revisits in another poem, that 'calcination' never destroys the primary metals which have nourished it—nor was this his wish. Throughout his writing career, beyond the seductive lures of the imagination—of metaphors, myths, dreams, pictures or fantasies—he always upheld the terse dictum of Wallace Stevens: 'Bare earth is best'. As Bonnefoy would have it, when all is said and done, the only thing that makes us human is our finitude; and despite every other distraction, what shoulders the full weight of meaning in our lives is 'sheer reality, sufficient and without proof'. That summons—to exist completely and resolutely in this world—is his central message, and his enduring legacy to his readers. But this is not the place for an essay on Bonnefoy's *Together Still*, much less his oeuvre as a whole, so I will only touch on a few more points that may seem useful or intriguing.

As 'The Translator's Task' wittily lays out for us, nobody knew more about the ins and outs of translation than Yves Bonnefoy, one of the art's most signal practitioners. He would certainly have sympathized with one of my many quandaries about his text: it concerns 'And That, Again?'—the second poem of the sequence *Ursa Major*—where the French original mentions a *tortue*. The word can mean either 'turtle' or 'tortoise' in English;

and since the creature appears on a path—on the land rather than in the sea—it should properly be called a 'tortoise'. Yet the *tortue* in these lines has wings, which would tempt us to infer that Bonnefoy is mimicking the term 'turtledove', in a cross-linguistic play on words. As the pre-eminent translator of Shakespeare into French, he often alludes to the playwright—even importing phrases from his work directly in English (an enlivening facet of 'In the Artist's Studio', for example); and in previous poems, he has explicitly quoted Hamlet's 'quibbles' on the names of animals. So I have opted for 'turtle' here, as a tribute to Bonnefoy's rendition of *The Phoenix and the Turtle*, a cryptic love poem he may have had in mind while writing this one, which is equally mysterious.

Late in life, Bonnefoy went against his earlier habits by cultivating an unrhymed variant of the sonnet. This verse form is much less common in modern France than it has steadily remained in the English-speaking world, ever since Elizabethan times. Here again, we can surmise the influence of Shakespeare, all of whose sonnets the author beautifully rendered into French, sometimes in multiple versions. In *Together Still*, he gifts us his last sonnet cycle—and to my mind, his finest: *Ensemble la musique et le souvenir* (*Together Music and Memory*). Wordsworth was another of his guiding spirits, and the title recalls the English poet's assertion that poetry 'takes its origin from emotion recollected in tranquillity'. As to music, Bonnefoy has often emphasized the primacy of the aural element in verse. Inveterate readers of his work will also hear an overtone of Mahler, whose *Das Lied von der Erde* (*The Song of the Earth*) was one of his touchstones—especially the closing movement, 'Der Abschied' ('The Farewell'), in the poignant performance by Kathleen Ferrier. The first quatrain of the fourth sonnet subtly mirrors several of the Chinese verses the composer set to music, and the contralto's premature death may have sparked some of the imagery. But as with the persons and places previously adduced, it would be misguided to limit the scope of Bonnefoy's sequence to such aspects alone. On the highest level, the 'voice' he aims to invoke is the creative act; and once the latter has ended, 'song' becomes autonomous: poetry itself, eternally re-enacting its own birth.

As in all his other books, throughout *Ensemble encore* we come across those elusive words that have confounded the poet's translators for decades: *évidence* ('self-evidence', or more often—according to Bonnefoy, as he told me long ago—'reality pure and simple'); *biens*, variously transposed as 'belongings' or 'good things', in order to retain the accent on *le bien* ('the good'); and *nuée*, an old word for 'cloud', but which currently connotes a mass of clouds moving across the sky. Nor should we forget the word *invisible*, with its difficult cadence for English verse; to tether a rhythm, I have rendered it once in these pages as 'unseen'—yet in the lofty sense of *visibilium et invisibilium*, 'the seen and the unseen'. The *coupe* or 'cup' that figures so strongly in the opening and closing poems of the collection seems to vary in function with the context: at times it resembles a ritual vessel, used for burning incense; at other times it appears to hold a liquid, the wine for a libation. Similarly, the word *fumée*, in the singular or plural, corresponds diversely to 'smoke' or 'vapour', drifting and dispersing even underwater. In the case of both *coupe* and *fumée*, flexibility must prevail in the translation, just as it does in the original.

The phrase '*Eo Romam*', mentioned at the end of the 'Bibliographic Notes', is usually cited as the response to the question '*Quo vadis?*' It occurs in the apocryphal book of the Acts of Peter. The poet's attribution of it to Virgil parallels a similar displacement in his autobiographical meditation, *L'Arrière-pays* (translated by Stephen Romer as *The Arrière-pays*, and also published by Seagull Books): a fruitful shift from the religious to the secular. Imaginatively, Bonnefoy has conflated the opening of the *Eclogues*, where the shepherds talk about Rome, with the scriptural passage. Those acquainted with his use of Christian legends in his writings, often borrowed from the iconography of Renaissance art, will perceive the alchemical process at work yet again. By transmuting those myths—such as the banishment of Adam and Eve from Paradise, a recurrent theme in *Together Still*—he envelops the quotidian in a nimbus of the sacred, redefining the tenets of 'negative theology' in uniquely daring terms. Through an arduous self-discipline, focused on the *hic et nunc*, he disavows the illusions of divinity, even as he subsumes their gilded afterglow. Absent yet present, like the sun of Hopper's painting in the closing lines of *Poems for Truphémus*, they are 'light in an empty room'.

Sadly, I could no longer turn to Bonnefoy to answer my many queries, as he had so often done in the past. But I was more than pleased—overjoyed, in fact—that his daughter Mathilde agreed to field them. Of course, she knew many things I could not guess, such as the width of the *chemin* (whether 'path', 'lane' or 'road') in Warbende. Her renowned skill as a film editor stood us in good stead, as we constantly exchanged different 'takes' on the book, writing to each other from Brussels, Paris, Forlí, Venice, Athens, Berlin, Los Angeles or Santo Domingo. Cyberspace may be fraught with perils in other realms, but it does allow for the long-distance weaving, stitching and darning of a translated text. As we persisted at our joint revision for several months, I was increasingly impressed by her canny sensitivity to both languages, and her profound kinship with her father's oeuvre—from the inside. In all this painstaking effort, I felt that he was with us: that we were truly 'together still'.

Chief among the other friends who came to my aid was Anthony Rudolf, Bonnefoy's oldest living translator, the doyen of our far-flung band; his patience and acumen in accompanying me through the first stages of this project were nothing short of remarkable. I would also like to thank the Bonnefoy scholars Odile Bombarde and Patrick Labarthe for the light they shed on several conundrums. Nor should I omit to recall that in moments of doubt, Michele Casagrande, Lena Papadaki, Cécile Margellos and Pablo Baez lent me their loyal support. Like those of Mathilde Bonnefoy, I have greatly valued all these contributions—though it goes without saying that any flaws in the translation, and in this afterword, are solely my own.

Over several years, long before the publication of *Ensemble encore*, Yves Bonnefoy sent me early versions of many of the poems that would eventually make up the collection. He expected that—as usual—I would submit them to periodicals in the English-speaking world. As a result, initial drafts of some of these works have already appeared in the *New England Review*, *AGNI*, *Plume*, the *Seagull Catalogue*, and the *Fortnightly Review*. All are international journals that merit our sincere respect for sponsoring literature in translation. In addition, the first version of the Lisbon sonnet was included in the Festschrift honouring our mutual friend, the late Michael Sheringham of All Souls College, Oxford. Last but not least, several selections from this book will be published in the *Yves Bonnefoy Reader*, a two-volume anthology of the author's work slated to appear in 2017 and 2018 at the Carcanet Press.

My most heartfelt acknowledgment must naturally go to Yves Bonnefoy himself, for entrusting me with the translation of his poetic testament. Like the young man he conjures in 'Together Still', at the age of nineteen I also needed someone to have faith in me; and Bonnefoy consistently made that leap, year after year, whether I deserved it or not. In closing, I must also express my admiration for Naveen Kishore, the founder of Seagull Books, who has done more than anyone else to make the author's works available to the English-speaking public. Whether we are members of Bonnefoy's family, or his friends, translators, publishers and readers, we all join in looking back on his immense achievement with gratitude and awe. Throughout his long and productive life, he selflessly refined the letter of his writings, in order to bequeath to us a lasting spiritual gold. Even in these final months, as *Together Still* attests, though 'the voice was dying, song had given birth'.

Hoyt Rogers